GREATNESS

OUR CALL TO A MAGNIFICENT AND MAGNANIMOUS LIFE

SELIKEM AKONDO

Copyright © Selikem Akondo
All Rights Reserved.

This book has been published with all efforts taken to make the material error-free after the consent of the author. However, the author and the publisher do not assume and hereby disclaim any liability to any party for any loss, damage, or disruption caused by errors or omissions, whether such errors or omissions result from negligence, accident, or any other cause.

While every effort has been made to avoid any mistake or omission, this publication is being sold on the condition and understanding that neither the author nor the publishers or printers would be liable in any manner to any person by reason of any mistake or omission in this publication or for any action taken or omitted to be taken or advice rendered or accepted on the basis of this work. For any defect in printing or binding the publishers will be liable only to replace the defective copy by another copy of this work then available.

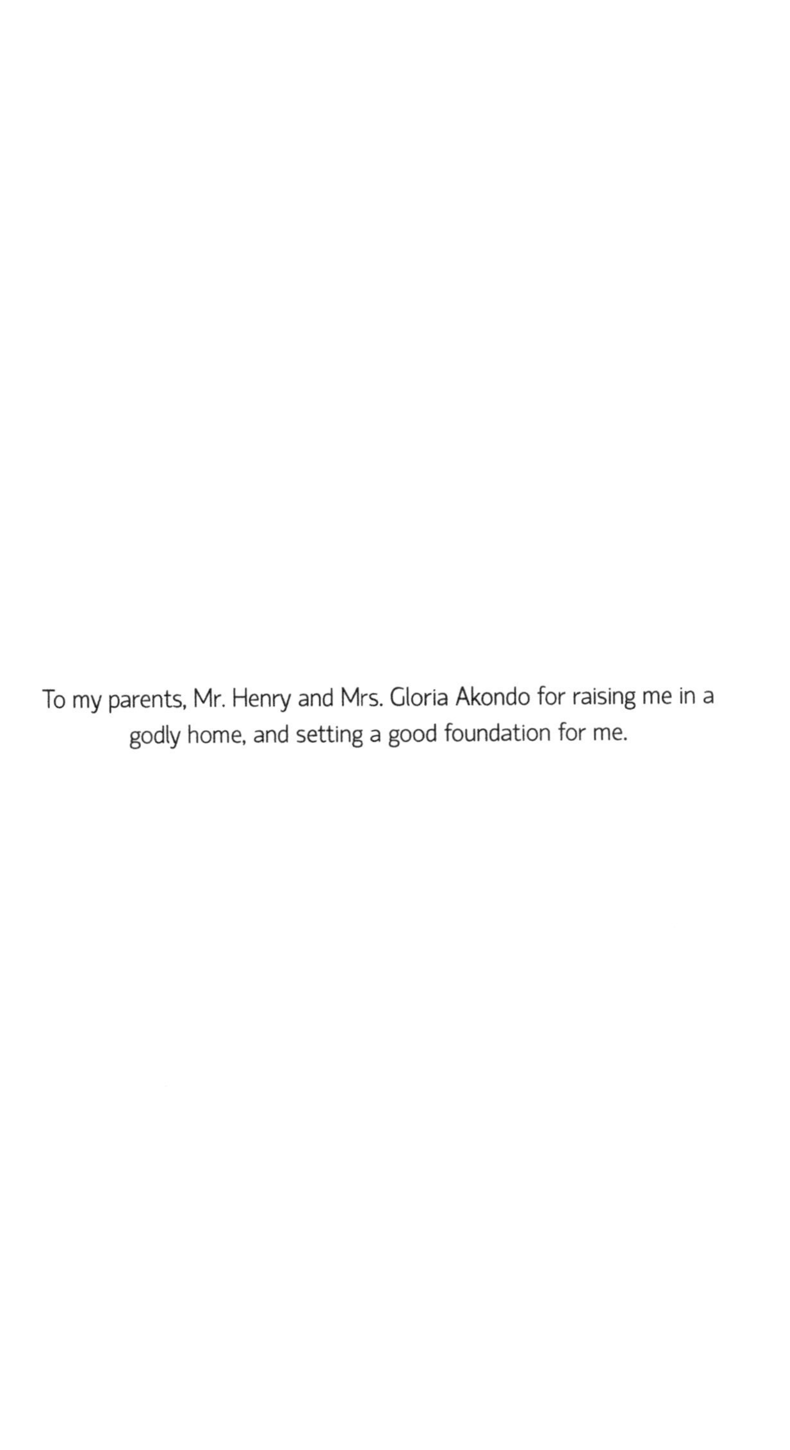

To my parents, Mr. Henry and Mrs. Gloria Akondo for raising me in a godly home, and setting a good foundation for me.

Contents

Acknowledgements *vii*

Foreword *ix*

Preface *xi*

1. Chapter 1 1
2. Chapter 2 9
3. Chapter 3 19
4. Chapter 4 28
5. Chapter 5 33

Conclusions 39

Acknowledgements

Profound gratitude goes to God Almighty who has sustained and given me grace to work on this first book. To him be all the glory.

Mrs. Rosebud Facor, thank you for your motherly love, prayers, encouragement and support all these years. You are dearly loved and cherished.

Sisters: to my older sister, Selase, you have been a great pacesetter and an inspirer. I always learn from you when we talk. You motivated me to write this book. God bless you. To my younger sister, Adeline, what can I say, my go to person for checks and balances, your input in this book is phenomenal; reading through manuscripts, helping choose book cover etc., is greatly appreciated.

Rev Dickson Tuffour Sarpong: thank you for your great impact in my life. I would need volumes of pages to write about you, however, I would like to say I truly appreciate you. I really do.

Prophet Christopher Yaw Annor. From afar you drew me closer. I found new hope and life by meeting you. Your words of encouragement, prayer and leadership has brought me thus far. I am most grateful.

Rev. Anthony Cudjoe: for your spiritual instruction and oversight. I appreciate you Sir.

Apostle Dr. John Kpikpi. I appreciate you so much Sir. For your words of wisdom, wealth of knowledge and great input in my life. As your mentee I have learned both from afar and near how you conduct your life, family and ministry and the great achievements you have today. I am inspired by your life story, and it is one reason I determined to work and finish this book. I am eternally grateful Sir.

Dr. Charles J Buckman, a father, mentor, inspirer, motivational surgeon. Since I had an encounter with him in 2015 at a relationship seminar in Koforidua, I have never ceased to follow and receive insightful teaching from him; you have genuinely taken keen interest of me; calling (even when in England), advising and praying for me. When in Ghana, I am among the first people you call to come over to your residence for us to just "hang out" while impacting nuggets of life to me. You have given me exposure through your radio, TV, and speaking engagements you've invited me to (both in Accra and Cape Coast). You inspired me to work on this piece. You have been there for me in ways I cannot fully state here because of space. Thank you, Daddy.

Rev. Albert Ocran, who charged me to write a book when he came to minister the word of God to us at the Legon Campus Ministry in 2013. You told me specifically to, "write a book in the next four years" Those words kept ringing in my ears and today the first work is out.

Mrs. Adjei-Brobbey for your contribution and inputs, greatly cherished and appreciated.

A special thank you to Pastor Thompson Afari who preached the word powerfully for me to give my life to Christ on September 4th, 2005.

And to all my cherished teachers, friends, colleagues and family members who have contributed directly or indirectly towards my development in life thus far. God richly bless and make you all greater than you are today!

Foreword

The call for us to be fruitful is a basic principle for growth. It comes from a place of potential being harnessed so that the substance of what lies deep within springs out with a flourish. The fruit by itself is beautiful to look at, savor and cherish. If taken as is, it is an adorning grace and pride, a symbol of achievement, a presentation of "I have arrived". In the fruit form, it gladdens the heart and glorified evidence to look at and rejoice with the achiever, so it has arrived with such beauty, but it stands alone. It has no impact on the environment it stands in and contribute nothing to it. Soon, everything else around it begins to die, a desert is formed around it and with one evil wind or fire or storm, it is blown away and dies out.

The fruit had the potential to have averted this situation simply by sharing and sowing its own potentials it carried in it a seed, which if shared could have birth another tree, and the tree will have born more fruits and the fruits will have borne more trees and soon a forest of good trees with a perpetual increase will have been established. The increase through multiplication of itself will have stood against every wind, storm, or fire because it had the potential to replenish itself.

You can achieve all that you are born to be with the right attitude and mindset. This is the principle God established for men when he gave the command in Genesis: 1:28" Be fruitful, multiply and replenish the earth". By ourselves we can achieve and be adorned. By our growth and increase we multiply and become a force against every evil wind, storm, or fire.

This book encourages you not to deem yourself lowly but to take up the challenge to develop yourself, to be fruitful, take territory and multiply. It is a call for you to manifest that which God called you to be and made you to become. I encourage you to read it and rise to the challenge.

Dr. Anthony Seddoh
Presiding Minister, Camp Elim
Accra, Ghana

Preface

Greatness, what it is

The price of greatness is responsibility.

Winston Churchill

You may have heard of the word greatness on several occasions and have probably used it in conversations with other people, or perhaps, with yourself. Greatness is not a new word to many people, especially in our days where almost every young person is expected to excel and be outstanding in several ways. You are likely to hear a young person being told "You have to be great", "To be great, do this and that", and sometimes, the strong word of caution that can put you on your toes: "You won't be great with this lifestyle you have started". There are many people cheering us on to greatness. The examples of people believed and known to be great whom we are usually expected to look up to are enormous.

Often, you would hear people say things such as, "May we be great", "That is a great leader" or "That child is going to be great someday". We say it. We hear it. And sometimes, we even claim to feel greatness coming our way. We could snap our fingers and scream, "The year is gonna be great" knowing that there are a lot of good things ahead. And if I asked if you would want to be great, I'm sure your response would be loud and very affirmative, "Yes, of course, I want to be great." I'd say the same too. Greatness is a good thing and almost everybody would want to be associated with it. Many words immediately come to mind when we hear the word greatness; success, achievement, excellence, influence, power, and fame. Usually, these are words that make us feel important. Hardly would you meet someone you wouldn't want to be great or be identified with greatness. What then is greatness? Is it something we can perceive or guess we would have or become? Do those words mean truly mean greatness? Can we work on it? Do we all have what it takes to be great or are some made to be great? The questions on greatness seem endless.

Perspectives on greatness

The Oxford Learner's Dictionaries define greatness as "*The quality of being extremely good in ability or quality and therefore admired by many people*".

Thus, if this definition is anything to go by, you could assess a person's performance and conclude if they would be great or not. This gives the impression that greatness can be looked at in the light of success. In other words, if a person is successful or prominent, then from this perspective, that individual is great.

For James Ray, an American author and life coach, greatness is "*The ability to achieve what you choose to achieve in the area you choose to achieve it; and to achieve it with excellence and a level of mastery.*"

Dictionary.com also defines greatness as "*the quality or state of being important, notable, or distinguished*". With this in view, influential people like politicians, celebrities, renowned authors, business men and other known public figures are referred to as great people. In History, some individuals are touted as great men and women because of the achievements they made. Some of them, by being famous alone, have registered themselves in the books of great people. It is no doubt that greatness is sought after by many individuals. It is presented as a means to winning the hearts of many and or getting uncommon recognition or opportunities, making one easily admirable and noticeable among many and it is a great thing to be associated with.

And in some instances, making life relatively easier for those great people.

William Shakespeare, an English playwright, poet and actor believed *"Some are born great, some achieve greatness, and some have greatness thrust upon them"*.

The Bible's perspective of Greatness

Contrary to what the world perceives as great, the Bible reveals that greatness is not only accomplishments and acquisition of materials by the efforts of man. It is also not necessarily becoming famous or successful in the world's view. The Bible teaches greatness as a nature of God deposited in man to excel and fulfill his purpose. It is not only about the possessions one acquires, but also the richness of a person's personality; character and charisma. That means that man's greatness is tied to God's greatness. Man can be great because of the greatness of God in him. Man can be great because the Great God enables him to. Thus, every man, regardless of race, colour, belief, educational qualification, level of spirituality, faith, gender or physique can be great because he is created in the image and likeness of God. You can be great. It is possible. It is not just to cheer you, but for you to believe and walk in it. Greatness is in you. All you have to do is to unleash every potential that God, the creator, has deposited in you. Look to Him and know that you have greatness in you and do great things just as He does.

The Etymology of Greatness

The Latin root word magn means "great." This root word is the origin of quite a number of English vocabulary words, including magnificent, magnitude, and magnanimous. An easy way to remember that magn means "great" is through the word magnifying glass, which makes something small "great" in size. The magnifying glass is a scientific instrument that makes something small appear bigger, in other words, "great" so as to be seen more easily and visibly. Other scientific instruments such as telescopes also use a similar principle or concept. They are used in the magnification of smaller, invisible, distant objects to become more real and visible to a viewer.

Thus, we say the small object has become great. By application, we allude that God is the magnifying glass in whose eyes we should see small things as great.

Magnificent and Magnanimous Defined

The word greatness is derived from these two words magnificent and magnanimous. Magnificent basically means making great, that is, in terms of function.

Magnanimous on the other hand is derived from two words: "magnus" which means great and "animus" which means soul. Therefore, magnanimous means great soul, big-hearted, in terms of personality.

So in life, sometimes, we begin from a small, insignificant place, but that should not be our stopping place, that should not deter or prevent us from becoming what God has called us to become; to be like Him here on earth—for you are a chosen generation, a royal priesthood, a holy people, called forth to show the glory, power, excellence and eminence of our God. Again, our calling requires that as He is, so should we be here on earth. The Bible declares the whole world is waiting for the manifestation of the sons of God. That's amazing! The earth is waiting for you to become all that God has made for you. It is waiting for me, too. I am eager to see the manifestation of God's greatness exhibited or revealed through the sons and daughters of God including you, yes you reading this book right now. Greatness is in you! Now, can we talk about the Greatness of God for a minute?

CHAPTER ONE

The Greatness of God

*O LORD, how great are Your works! Your thoughts are very deep [**Psalm 92:5**].*

God is great. This is a very simple and popular truth you would hear or read in many circles. It is simple but pregnant with a lot of insights for man. A lot of people acknowledge that the creator of the universe is great. Indeed, God is. The greatness of God surrounds man because God has made it so. But what does His greatness mean, and how do we know the magnitude of His greatness?

When the Bible talks of God's greatness, it usually draws our attention to two main truths or two ways we can understand it. The first truth of God's greatness is that **God is great in His personality**. That is who he is. It is not just one of His attributes; that is the totality of his being. He is great. He is mighty and wields so much power that nobody can comprehend. He has a lot of good and wonderful things in Him that amaze men; love, generous, mighty, all-powerful, all-knowing, wonderful and a whole lot. Throughout the Bible, we see how the greatness of God in his personality is highly spoken of.

In **Nehemiah 13:22** *"...Remember to me, my God, this also, and spare me according to the greatness of your loving kindness"*, the Bible talks of the greatness of God's loving-kindness. Other scriptures talk of the greatness of His power (Psalms 79:1), acts (Psalms 150:2), name (Jeremiah 10:6, Joshua 7:9, 1 Samuel 12:22), excellence (Exodus 15:7) and His strength (Isaiah 40:26).

The second way the greatness of God is known is through the things he does, His function. He does great things. He has not concealed his greatness in his personality alone, He has also made it visible through his works so that even without getting to know Him on a personal level to acknowledge His personality, man can from afar or a distance, know of His greatness. Without knowing the greatness of His loving-kindness or mercies or riches, we can behold His creation and see His greatness. Thus, God's greatness is visible in the things he does; His creation, acts of goodness and mercies, love and the blessings He bestows on man. He is a great king.

Psalm 111:2

Great are the works of the LORD; they are pondered by all who delight in them.

The Bible is full of mighty acts of God that tell us how great He is (Psalm 111:2, 80:10, 86:8-10, Jeremiah 10:12). In the Psalms, many songs and poems are written to portray this. The people of old saw God move. They saw Him do awesome things that other gods couldn't do, even with all their powers and fame. God Almighty, with even the minutest of His actions, reveals His greatness. He parted the red sea for the Israelites to pass through, healed their bodies of sickness, did a lot of things that left many people wondering how that was possible. But God's great works do not end in the Old Testament. In the New Testament, we still see him on the go. He raised Jesus from the dead. That was a great move. Nobody had done that before. And Jesus still lives. In our days also, we are witnessing the mighty works of God in diverse ways. When Jesus came to earth, He demonstrated the greatness of God through His works. He taught with so much power and went about doing good works (Matthew 7:29, Mark 1:22, John 5:27, Luke 6:19).

I like that the Psalmist exclaims "*O Lord, how great are your works*"! It shows how amazed the Psalmist was. The Psalmist might have been dumbfounded by the things that God does. Sometimes, when we behold nature, how the skies and the mountains are well laid and beautifully designed, how man is "fearfully and wonderfully made", how God does so many things for us, we can agree with the Psalmist that God is great. We can also gladly exclaim O Lord, how great are your works!

Job 26:14 ESV

Behold, these are but the outskirts of his ways, and how small a whisper do we hear of him! But the thunder of his power who can understand?"

Job also, considering the works of God, acknowledged how great God is.

God doesn't only want to remain great. He also wants more of greatness to be seen through his creation. He wants His greatness to fill the entire earth in different fashions and styles.

Here's the catchy party of the story. Jesus said, "*Very truly I tell you, whoever believes in me will do the works I have been doing, and they will do even greater things than these, because I am going to the Father*" (**John 14:12**). That means your greatness can manifest if you believe. Jesus has assured us that we will do greater things. Isn't that amazing? You can be great because God approves it.

Say this with me, "I was born great. I will live great. I was born for greatness!"

In the creation story, we see how God made man like Him. When God was making man, he thought of greatness, He had in mind a people of His calibrewho would represent Him on earth and that is why He made us in His image and likeness. God did not make us helpless mortals who would wander on the earth and just die without making the most of our lives. He made us like Him. He gave us power, wisdom, strength, might, knowledge, talents, time and every other thing to display His greatness in us to the world. Let us go back to the creation story in the first book of the Bible where we get to see God at work.

26 Then God said, "Let Us make man in Our image, according to Our likeness, let them have dominion over the fish of the sea, over the birds of the air, and over the cattle, over all the earth and over every creeping thing that creeps on the earth."

27 So God created man in His own image; in the image of God. He created him; male and female He created them.

28 Then God blessed them, and God said to them, "Be fruitful and multiply; fill the earth and subdue it; have dominion over the fish of the sea, over the birds of the air, and over every living thing that moves on the earth." **(Genesis 1:26-28)**

God was very emphatic with the instructions He gave man at creation. Because God knew what man is made of, He pronounced that man should dominate over the "*fish of the sea, over the birds of the air, and over the cattle, over all the earth and over every creeping thing that creeps on the earth*". Man is only able to do this because of the nature of God in him. He was made in the image and likeness of God. We have said that God is great in personality, so is man created to be. God is great in the things He does, such is how man was weird to operate.

In essence, every man has the potential to be great. Unfortunately, not everybody is living up to the potential and greatness in them. Some people have bought the argument that there are people who are born great and others aren't. Man's source is God. Regardless of who a person is, where he is born or raised, he can rise to greatness if he holds on to the truth that God has made him in His image and likeness and acts accordingly.

Why should we strive for greatness?

We are indeed made of a great God. When He made us, He poured out himself into us so that we can become like Him on earth. He made us in His image and likeness. Nothing can change it. But a lot can happen if we fail to walk in this truth. A lot more can also happen if we walk in the realisation of what we are made of. We see Him in us. Yet, that doesn't automatically make our greatness visible for men to behold. The greatness of God is a seed in us, a personality or potential deposited in us that we can unearth.

When God made Adam and Eve, He made a profound statement that shouldn't be taken lightly. In the Garden of Eden, God ordered Adam and Eve to be "fruitful and multiply and replenish the earth". That was a dominion mandate he gave man. That doesn't also mean that just by being human, you will walk in greatness. No. That is not the case. If you fold your arms and take no action, you remain the same. Your potential will be hidden in you and your generation will not taste of the goodness of God in you. You are made for more, don't settle for less. Pay the price and let your greatness manifest.

The price of greatness is responsibility - **Winston Churchill**

*28 Then God blessed them, and God said to them, "Be fruitful and multiply; fill the earth and subdue it; have dominion over the fish of the sea, over the birds of the air, and over every living thing that moves on the earth"***[Genesis 1:26-28]**.

All greatness is from God. He is the source of every great thing or great person, whether we acknowledge Him or not. Yes, some people are referred to as great and are not associated with God. The world celebrates many people as great who do not even believe in the existence of God. But whether they believe it or not, God is the creator of man and God's seed is in every man. They may not hold on to the truth in God's word but they may ignorantly or deliberately be living the principles of God that make a man great.

God is a God of principles. Inherent in His principles are keys that can make a man great. That notwithstanding, acknowledging His existence, walking in the truth of His word and honouring Him gives one an advantage in this world. God has enough to make everything or anyone great. As the source of greatness, it is not surprising that anyone who has a relationship with Him easily walks in greatness. If you have a relationship with God, you are at an advantage of becoming greater than someone who hasn't.

What it means to be fruitful

Fruitfulness is one the most preached and talked about subjects in Christianity. It is not only popular in Christianity; even atheists believe that man is supposed to be fruitful. When God made man and gave the instruction to be "fruitful and multiply", He wasn't just speaking on procreation, even though procreation is important to him and us as well. To be fruitful means to grow, blossom, and be productive. That means that man is not expected to retrogress, decrease or be stagnant. It is against God's order for man. If you find yourself living contrary to this truth, check it. All is not right, because you are defying the original intent of God for your life. God had knitted in man the ability to produce results that are beneficial and profitable. God's plan and expectation for man is to see man become great, just as He (God) is. Thus, man ought to be great in personality and function. Remember how He says it, "fill the earth". Fill the earth with your potential. Fill the earth with that dream. Fill the earth with your skills. It will be mediocre to limit one's self or domain to just a small portion of the earth when God has made available all you would need to reach the ends of the earth. So, with God, you can dream big because it is possible. He says fill the earth, not just a small portion you deem fit or where your imagination or expectation can reach. There are possibilities in God that can take a man to places beyond a small village or country or continent. With God, a man can reach the ends of the world with his greatness. This however does not mean that we will all become world-known or famous because of greatness. Our works, our potentials and our deeds can go beyond our comfort zones or places which are known. This suggests that our results can reach nations and people of different races.

Think of how God is known. Do you realize that He is not just coined in one small town or community? Though not every community or people will acknowledge Him the same way, it is no doubt that He is known in every part of the world. You can be known beyond your domain. If God instructs that we become fruitful and multiply, then it means that no matter what you possess, you can achieve greatness with it. You can multiply that little thing that sometimes seems irrelevant to become a difference-maker.

In God, something little can become great and bigger. In God's eyes, He sees greatness in every small thing. Begin to look at things from God's perspective and sooner than later you will begin acting and operating like this Magnanimous God.

CHAPTER TWO

The Seed of Greatness

Everyone has the power for greatness, not for fame, but greatness, because greatness is determined by service

Martin Luther King Jr.

I want to be great, and I know you want to be, too. The goal of life for many people is to become better and achieve something substantial with their lives. They realise there is a version of themselves they haven't become yet, there is an unquenchable thirst to achieve something or become something better. Many times, the conclusion is; we want to be great. Call it success, call it achievement or accomplishments, call it purpose or fulfilment. For many people, greatness is something to be associated with, regardless of how valid or invalid their perception of greatness is. Man's longing for greatness is natural. We are born into this world with that desire to be more than we see around us or experience. Without much effort, we see our hearts yearning for greatness. In Mike Bickle's book, *The Seven Longings of the Human Heart*, he says that *"It is not bad to desire to be great, but how we go about it is what matters"*. Because there is a tainted picture of greatness in the world today, you can find yourself pursuing vanity all in the name of greatness or wanting to be great.

Greatness comes from God. Humans are wired with the desire to be great because there is a seed of greatness deposited in everyone that makes us bold and confident to desire greatness. It is not only about your exposure, experience, or examples that give the desire, but it is about what is in you. You don't always need the best of education and experiences to be great, even though education is important. Somewhere in a remote community, a young boy or girl who has very little knowledge of who the world's greatest people are or what his or her peers are achieving in other parts of the world, or doesn't even know what greatness is, is somehow longing to be great. In their mind's eye, there is more beyond what exists around them. Without education, exposure or experience, their hearts long for something beyond their environment.

That is also not to say that exposure, experience and the examples of others are irrelevant in our quest for greatness. What these things do is stir what is already in us. So we see or read of great people such as Kwame Nkrumah, Nelson Mandela Aliko Dangote, Desmond Tutu, Napoleon Bonaparte, Alexander the Great, Martin Luther King and the rest and we leap with joy. Our desires intensify because, indirectly, we get a way or standard to measure our dream to be great. Sometimes, we get examples to challenge us.

We have established that when God made man, He poured himself into man. God's greatness in man is like a seed that can grow into a tree and bear fruit. Just as a little seed can grow into a mighty tree so can a desire of greatness manifest mightily. When seeds are planted, as little and fragile as they are, sometimes, they develop roots and then sprout out of the soil regardless of the resistance that could come their way and form a tree.

Becoming Great

Although greatness is like a seed, its manifestation takes a while. It is a process. And that means it doesn't happen overnight. Little by little, you would chalk a lot of success in that journey. Nobody wakes up one day from sleep and becomes great. There is a process; working at what you're doing and who you are to become what you are destined to be. You can't just pick a seed and show it around as a valuable asset. In its state as a seed, it is sometimes of little value to anyone who sees it. You don't see what it is made of. It becomes great when it has evolved from that stage. A seed is more beneficial when it has matured into a tree that can produce fruit, else, it would lose its value. Even the people whose greatness look sudden or unexpected to others did not wake up on a good day and became great. It took time and work to become great. It is the manifestation that occurred suddenly.

Key Elements You Need To Manifest Your Greatness

1. **Mindset**

Just as the name suggests, mindset is how you set or position thoughts or ideas in your mind. What you set your mind on. The things you allow your mind to dwell on are what form a mindset. Mindsets are developed when a person holds on to beliefs and thoughts that inform how they view the world around them. We all have it. We have our perception about things because of what we know or do not know or even what we have experienced. It influences everything we do in life; thoughts, feelings, reactions, and responses. Your habits are also a product of your mindset.

There are people whose position on finance is that money is the root of all evil. They don't want to make more money or have enough to meet their needs; that is their mindset. It informs their financial decisions and even how they approach anything money-related. It is the same with greatness too. A person's mindset can make them mediocre in life or great. If you hold on to the belief that some people are born great and others are not, you can be reluctant and approach life casually as though nothing is at stake. But something will be affected if you don't become great. People will be deprived of the benefits of your greatness and God will not be glorified in your life. You can become great if you realise that you have what it takes to be. The seed of greatness is in you. Note this, it also doesn't end at the realisation. It is only a part of the process, not the end.

A mindset can be changed, grown, or improved. You become what you constantly think about, that is the power of thoughts. If you are constantly thinking about negative things, it will be difficult for you to achieve anything positive. Your mindset will inform every critical decision concerning you. Thus, it is very essential to have a greatness mindset; the mindset to take small, insignificant things, expand them and make them magnificent—see them become bigger, better and greater. A greatness mindset does not accept and settle for smallness. People with a greatness mindset don't condone mediocrity.

To become great, have a growth mindset. A mindset that propels you and opens you to improve because you realise that as the seed of greatness is in you, many possibilities can come into fruition. Having this mentality gives you a foundation to build on. You have a solid foundation, one that cannot be defeated.

Remember what the Word of God says *"As he thinketh in his heart, so is he"* – **Proverbs 23:7.** Your thoughts matter!

Mindset That Can Prevent Greatness

A. **Comparison**

Sometimes, when you see a beautiful painting on the wall, you can stand in awe of how talented the artist is. You know you couldn't have done that. Maybe if you tried, you wouldn't be that good. How about the admiration for that singer who is able to hit all the high notes and whose singing gives you goose pimples? It is no doubt, we admire people who seem to be incredibly good at what they do. People who are doing incredible things in their fields or areas of specialization can easily win our hearts. We can look at their works, personalities and downplay what we are or have.

No two individuals are the same. Our intellect, perception, physical appearance, beliefs and dreams are different. Our differences are what make each person unique in their own way. It is easy to get carried away by other people's uniqueness. We admire how they do certain things effortlessly. The admiration even intensifies when we struggle to do the things they do. Nothing should prevent us from admiring and acknowledging the uniqueness and achievements of other people. Nevertheless, it should not become a tool for comparison which can breed inferiority complex or bitterness. Comparison is a mindset that hinders greatness. You are unique! There is something that distinguishes you from other people. You may not be a good singer like a fellow in the choir, but you have something that makes you stand out. People who keep comparing themselves to others never achieve anything great. That person has the seed of greatness and so do you. Don't have the mindset of unhealthy comparison. Value what you are and strive to become great. You are made by a great God. There is greatness in you, believe it and live it.

A. **People's perception**

When your self-worth is all from what other people think of you, you may never be great. Great people don't fully hold on to other people's perceptions of them. People can be wrong, biased, or unfair in the perception they have about you. **What people think of you is not always the truth!** Becoming great requires that you believe in yourself more than what others think. Though you can't entirely ignore what people think of you, you shouldn't also hold that as truth. Great people don't seek validation of themselves from other people. That is not the mindset of greatness. Remember that "*No matter what other people think of you at any particular moment, one thing is certain – you're never as good or bad as they say you are*" - **Travis Bradberry.**

C. **Fear**

Nothing has stopped many people from becoming great more than fear. Fear of the unknown, fear of failure, fear of what people will say, fear of death, fear of this and that and the list keeps going on and on. Fear is a negative emotion that prevents many people from becoming great. We experience it in our minds but we can see its impact in the physical. Many times, you can't even hide it. Fear can make you make shy away from opportunities that can launch you into your season of manifestation. Sometimes, it can even make you mess up when given the opportunity. Fear has indeed robbed many people. Don't be the next victim. Though fear is a strong opponent, it is not stronger than you are. Fear can be defeated. You can win the battle over fear. Fear is a choice you make. Shun this negative mindset and think of greatness.

2. **Posture**

Another element we need in manifesting greatness is our posture. This is not the physical position in which someone holds their body when standing or sitting. A posture is an attitude, approach or position you have towards something. So, we can take a cue from the physical posture, how you can position yourself for a purpose. Here, it is a conscious mental or outward behavioral attitude towards a subject. Your approach to life and the experiences that come with it matters. To become great, recognize that your posture is in line with what God has for you. Your position towards the process of greatness should not be negative. It won't always be smooth, rosy, promising and easy, but our approach to it can influence our manifestation. Have a positive posture.

3. **Claim God's promises**

There are many promises God has for you in His word. They are yours but if you do not know and take possession of them, you won't enjoy those promises. Greatness is first of all in God. He has deposited it in us like a seed that can bear many fruits. Not only has God done that, but He has also prepared the way for us to walk smoothly in this journey. As part of that, He has given specific words concerning our lives. But how do we get to know the promises of God for us? His word. His promises are in His word. You can't get a hold of them if you don't enjoy time in His word. Reading His word will give knowledge of the promises He has for you, but it doesn't end there. If you stop at reading and knowing alone, you will miss out on the most important thing-enjoying it. The goal of the promises is to make life better. Claim those promises and see them in your life.

Here are some of the promises of God you can claim. He said He will make you great. Only believe and watch Him fulfil what he has said.

And I will make of thee a great nation, and I will bless thee, and make thy name great; and thou shalt be a blessing:

Genesis 12:2

And the LORD said to her: "Two nations are in your womb, Two peoples shall be separated from your body; One people shall be stronger than the other, And the older shall serve the younger."

Genesis 25:23

For the LORD thy God blesseth thee, as he promised thee: and thou shalt lend unto many nations, but thou shalt not borrow; and thou shalt reign over many nations, but they shall not reign over thee.

Deuteronomy 15:6

"And all nations will call you blessed, For you will be a delightful land," Says the LORD of hosts.

Malachi 3:12

4. Determination

The story of greatness is never complete without determination. Throughout the Bible to our current dispensation, great people have always fought against all odds to be what they were. Great people have one thing in common and that is determination. To become great, you have to be determined. Merriam Webster's dictionary defines determination as "*A quality that makes you continue trying to do or achieve something that is difficult".* Your greatness may delay or be concealed if you are not determined enough. Determination is like fuel. It keeps you going. Yes, God has said you will be great but many forces will fight you. They will be negative thoughts, toxic people, tough times, attacks and a lot that can demotivate you. Determination is what will be the game-changer for you.

5. **Obedience to God**

Your obedience to God is key to your greatness as an individual. Obedience requires that you heed the instructions of God concerning your life. For everyone, God has a clear purpose and plan for their lives. These plans are not to restrain us but rather make it easier for us to be on the path to greatness. Identifying the purpose is important but the more important thing is to discover the plan for the fulfilment of the purpose and obey Him every step of the way. Disobedience can cause you a lot.

6. **Provide Solutions**

Great people are problem solvers. The ability to provide solutions is what distinguishes ordinary men from extraordinary men. In a world where there are more problems and challenges, it is only the men who pay the price to make the lives of people and the society at large better who become great. Find a problem around you and provide the solution. That is what will make you great. You have potential in you. You have ideas and wield so much power to cause a positive change. The world is waiting for your manifestation. Let the seed of greatness in you come out. You of the Great One, show it.

Have you got your key elements ready?

CHAPTER THREE

God's Great People of The Bible

"There is no one who is insignificant in the purpose of God" – **Alistair Begg**

The Bible is filled with some very dramatic and straightforward stories of many men and women who were used by God for mighty things. Some kings and queens who stood out among their peers in biblical accounts. Other great people in the Bible were seen in the military and war front, priesthood, i.e., prophets and preachers of God, stewardship, leadership, rulership and others. Some of these people demonstrated excellence in their respective endeavours and showed God's greatness in them. They have since become examples for many people even after several years of their death. Many of these great people of God we talk about can be seen as major characters in the stories told about them. That doesn't mean that to be great, one has to necessarily be in the limelight. It is possible to be great even if you are not famous or in the limelight. So like the words of Ina D. Ogdon's **Brighten the Corner Where You Are**, you can make significant contributions to humanity regardless of where you are.

Do not wait until some deed of greatness you may do,
Do not wait to shed your light afar;
To the many duties ever near you now be true,
Brighten the corner where you are.

Refrain:
Brighten the corner where you are!
Brighten the corner where you are!
Someone far from harbour you may guide across the bar;
Brighten the corner where you are!

You can be less seen yet be great in the midst of people who are touted as famous, known, popular and successful. Greatness can be realised anywhere and in any position. What you need to do is make good use of what you have; the gifts and talents, and fulfil your purpose.

Now, let's delve into the lives of great men and women of God in the Bible.

ABRAHAM

Till today, Abraham is known as the father of many nations. Abraham was a man whose story and walk with God showed how great God was. His story has many parts and in putting the pieces together, you would realize why he registered his name in the Bible as one of the great men of God regardless of his imperfection. In his book, *Life Sentences*, Dr. Warren. W. Wiersbe claims, "*Next to our Lord Jesus Christ, perhaps the greatest example of faith in Scripture is the patriarch Abraham.*"

Abraham lived an exemplary life of giving his heart to God and His work, such that even when God instructed him to offer his only son, Isaac, whom he had waited many years to have, he didn't grumble or complain, but in all submission, acted as the Lord had asked. He was willing to give his all to the Lord without withholding anything. He was ready to die empty. Are you willing to do that? Would you go the length Abraham did? Abraham was a man whose faith was tested but he didn't fail. He obeyed to the end. Not many people will be willing to make a move like Abraham did. He was a man who listened to God and acted in faith.

By myself I have sworn, declares the Lord, because you have done this and have not withheld your son, your only son, I will surely bless you, and I will surely multiply your offspring as the stars of heaven and as the sand that is on the seashore. And your offspring shall possess the gate of his enemies, and in your offspring shall all the nations of the earth be blessed, because you have obeyed my voice.

– Genesis 22:16-18

Abraham's obedience is not all there is to him. He is also known for leadership in his family. Though he had Isaac in his old age, Abraham demonstrated leadership in his family life. He was a leader by example and showed love and care for his family. Interestingly, the word love was first used in reference to Abraham's affection for Isaac. Isn't that a great way to live? Like Abraham, there may be a peculiar assignment for you in your family, you can be great in that space too. Lead with diligence and portray the excellence of God the Father.

Abraham was always building an altar for the LORD at every promise he received from Him. That was also one of the things that made him stand out. He endeavoured to keep the promises of God in remembrance.

[Genesis 13:14-17]

14 And the LORD said to Abram, after Lot had separated from him: "Lift your eyes now and look from the place where you are—northward, southward, eastward, and westward; 15 for all the land which you see I give to you and your descendants forever. 16 And I will make your descendants as the dust of the earth; so that if a man could number the dust of the earth, then your descendants also could be numbered. 17 Arise, walk in the land through its length and its width, for I give it to you.

It is important to note that these things made Abraham great because, in the days of Abraham, many people were not obedient to God. People pursued their desires and could barely wait for the duration Abraham did just to see a promise come true. Even today, many are still disobedient and impatient. Abraham teaches us a way to go. Abraham also gave himself unto prayer. Those are marks of a great man. Today, we also can fashion our lives after Abraham and learn from him to be great.

DAVID

For God to call a person *"a man after my heart"* (Acts 13:22) is staggering. That is a clue of how such a person lived. That must have been a life well lived! David started life as a shepherd boy; unpromising. There was little indication of him becoming a great personality whose descendants would later come to give birth to the saviour. God had already spoken some prophecies concerning him as the one who would rule over Israel but David didn't look it growing up. Maybe if we saw David in those days, we wouldn't associate greatness with him either. A shepherd boy who was known for either looking after his sheep or playing music, living a very simple life, but David worked towards greatness even from his days as a shepherd boy to the throne. With much resilience, David rose from the position of a shepherd boy to become a saviour of Israel, killing the Goliath and claiming victory for the people. David, while a shepherd, was very committed to his work. He loved his work and did it excellently. It wasn't any special work like working in the king's palace or working as an official, yet David approached his task with passion. Guarding the flock, leading the sheep, protecting them at the detriment of his own life. Shepherding was tough work, very time demanding and risky, sometimes.

"The LORD who delivered me from the paw of the lion and from the paw of the bear will deliver me from the hand of this Philistine" **(1 Samuel 17)**.

The story of David and Goliath is widely known among many Christians. As a boy, David demonstrated the greatness of God by exhibiting courage in the face of a tough opposition that many of the Israelites feared, Goliath. Let us go back and reflect on God's greatness. God is great in person and in deeds. David demonstrated greatness in his personality just as God does. David acted fearlessly and confidently and won victory over the Philistines. He channelled his expertise in shepherding into winning victory. That was wisdom on display.

48 As the Philistine moved closer to attack him, David ran quickly toward the battle line to meet him. 49 Reaching into his bag and taking out a stone, he slung it and struck the Philistine on the forehead. The stone sank into his forehead, and he fell facedown on the ground.

50 So David triumphed over the Philistine with a sling and a stone; without a sword in his hand he struck down the Philistine and killed him.

51 David ran and stood over him. He took hold of the Philistine's sword and drew it from the sheath. After he killed him, he cut off his head with the sword.

When the Philistines saw that their hero was dead, they turned and ran.

1 Samuel 17:48-51

David eventually becomes a leader of Israel (1 Samuel 16:13) and chalks many successes in his tenure of office. He demonstrated courage, loyalty, and success as the King of Israel who won many battles for the Lord.

The life of David, though full of dramatic events, tells of how greatness can be realized in a man. David had a humble beginning as a young boy but his knowledge and walk with God made it possible for him to birth the greatness in him. He never despised himself. He recognized the God he served and was confident in him. He knew how God would transform his skills as a shepherd to victory for the Israelites and he acted accordingly.

Even as a leader, David showed mercy and compassion towards many people. This act was vital to his success as king. Greatness is also seen in relationships with others because relationships are important to living a purposeful life. God is rich in mercy and loving-kindness. He shows mercy to whom He wants to, and that is one of the things that make Him great. David also showed mercy to Saul.

"The LORD forbid that I should do such a thing to my master, the LORD's anointed, or lay my hand on him; for he is the anointed of the LORD."

1 Samuel 24:6

David's greatness doesn't imply that he was flawless. He had his setbacks as an individual. Even as a king, he faulted in the sight of God but remains one of the Bible characters who lived a great life. Your setbacks or weaknesses do not mean that you cannot be great. David was great and so are you. You are made for greatness. Your present situation is not all there is to your life. Like David, recognize the God you serve, acknowledge what skills or situations you find yourself in, and seek wisdom to make good out of it. That could be the beginning of writing your story of greatness. It won't be easy. The opposition will come your way just as David witnessed, but don't let it take hold of you. You are on an assignment to become the great man or woman you are made to become. Don't stop here.

1. **NEHEMIAH**

In the history of rebuilding the temple of God, the name Nehemiah will always remain. What leadership! "*A rather ordinary person in a servant position, became a transformational leader when apprised of the discontent of the post exilic Jews in Jerusalem and Judah*" *as* Cheryl Patton puts it. That is greatness over there. He had only returned from exile in Persia by the Persian King Artaxerxes I to Jerusalem after he was released. Nehemiah rose from the position of a royal cupbearer to the governor of Judah who ensured that the broken walls of Jerusalem were built. He is known throughout history as a great leader.

In the story of Nehemiah's greatness, we see how strategies like prayer made him a leader with a difference, such that even today, modern-day leadership can be modelled after him. He was always praying to God for the temple to be built. He prayed for the Lord to give him a vision. He looked to God to make the building possible. He was far from having all the resources to build the temple for God, but he had determined to make it possible, come what may. He was a man who had complete faith in God and thus turned his focus to the Great One to help him. So, he resorted to prayer. And just prayer alone, he wailed. I can imagine the depth of passion he had. He couldn't hide his emotions. He was sad and it was written all over his face.

So it was, when I heard these words, that I sat down and wept, and mourned for many days; I was fasting and praying before the God of heaven. **Nehemiah 1:4**

For a man to seek the Lord's face with such brokenness is a sign of deep reverence for God. He also had a sorrowful heart and his deep concern showed all over his face. Nehemiah was in a position to be angry with the people. They seemed to have been negligent and unconcerned about it but he refused to thread that path. That situation is a replica of modern-day society; followers acting unconcerned and negligent. We see that all the time. Suffice to say that prayer is what made Nehemiah what he is known for today. A leader who prays is a great leader because he associates with the Great God.

Nehemiah showed concern without condemning others. God showed him mercy. He gained favour in the eyes of King Artaxerxes I whom he served. The king provided him escorts to Jerusalem and helped him acquire the materials he needed to rebuild the wall.

That was faith in motion. It didn't look possible that the temple could be rebuilt but Nehemiah stood up and travailed and proved to the people that it was possible. That is greatness. A great leader finds solutions to issues. Nehemiah did just that. He could have complained or grumbled like the others but he chose not to. He fasted, prayed and mourned for four months. That is a long period for a solo fast. He might have been weary at a point but he persevered.

4. JOSHUA

"Moses my servant is dead. Now then, you and all these people, get ready to cross the Jordan River into the land I am about to give to them—to the Israelites. I will give you every place where you set your foot, as I promised Moses."

Joshua 1:2-3

He was chosen to replace Moses in leading the Israelites to the promised land. As a boy, he had his own uncertainties about the call of God for him to lead the Israelites to the promised land, Canaan. But God always has a track record. He had been faithful to Moses, Joshua's predecessor and that was enough proof that He would be with Joshua. He assured him of His presence.

"Do not be afraid; do not be discouraged, for the Lord your God will be with you wherever you go."

Joshua 1:9

Like Joshua, many people today, have a fear of the unknown. What is ahead of us and how things will eventually unfold in the course of our lives. This man, Joshua, who was afraid, later became a great leader of great faith in God. His leadership over the Israelites was exemplary because of his faith. Joshua is known as one of the courageous leaders in the Bible. It was faithfulness and strong faith in God that made that possible for Him.

As a person, he was always willing to provide help to whoever needed it, regardless of whether he would benefit from it or not. When the Gibeonites were attacked by the Amorites and other nations, they came and asked for help from Joshua. Joshua immediately helped them, even though he had been deceived by them before.

Joshua became a great leader. He started as an ordinary man but his approach to his duties and conduct was not ordinary. Through praying, Joshua made history; the sun stooped in the middle of the sky. That is remarkable. Because of this, the Israelites were able to win victory over their enemies.

"On the day the LORD gave the Amorites over to Israel, Joshua said to the LORD in the presence of Israel: "Sun, stand still over Gibeon, and you, moon, over the Valley of Aijalon." So the sun stood still, and the moon stopped, till the nation avenged itself on its enemies, as it is written in the Book of Jashar. The sun stopped in the middle of the sky and delayed going down about a full day" **(Joshua 10: 12, 13)**.

The stories of God's great people are inspiring. Let's begin our journey to greatness.

CHAPTER FOUR

The Journey to Greatness

A journey of a thousand mile begins with a step – **Chinese Proverb**

Nobody becomes great in the twinkle of an eye. No. Not even the people whose greatness seem sudden to the world. The manifestation of your greatness could come as a surprise to people, but it is no proof that your greatness is sudden. Behind the scenes of your victory is a lot of toiling and working. It is the process and journeying you go through that many are oblivious of.

You won't wake up one morning and suddenly notice people acknowledging you for making significant contributions to society. Greatness has a beginning and journeys through to manifestation. It is a process. It is a journey. Let's consider the story of Joseph in the Bible. He was a young man who worked his way up to greatness. He was tending the flocks but people perhaps didn't see that as the beginning of greatness. Joseph was diligent as a shepherd from the time people couldn't see what he wouldbecome to the time his greatness became visible for all men to see.

"Joseph, a young man of seventeen, was tending the flocks...". **Genesis 37:2b**

Our lives are different, and maybe, unlike Joseph, we may not find ourselves in the position where we have a humble beginning of walking into greatness. So how do you know if you are on the path to greatness?

1. **Opposition**

If everybody is for you, then your greatness is still hidden in you. Great people face tough opposition. They face resistance, despicable people, enemies, setbacks and a lot of challenges simply because they want to remain unknown. Opposition is not something you would ordinarily like because it comes with discomfort and enmity. But it can also challenge you to move out of your comfort zone. Opposition is one thing that shows that you are journeying towards greatness. The path of greatness is not always smooth. There are setbacks, trials, rejection, discomfort and many other negative things that come with it. When you are doing something that can make you great, you'd face opposition. People would resist because you are striving to become extraordinary out of the masses. The story of Joseph is one of many that tell how opposition indicates greatness.

"When his brothers saw that their father loved him more than any of them, they hated him and could not speak a kind word to him".

"When he told his father as well as his brothers, his father rebuked him and said, "What is this dream you had? Will your mother and I and your brothers actually come and bow down to the ground before you?" **(Genesis 37:4, 10)**

Sometimes, you'd find relatives, friends, or even loved ones you look up to come against you because of the greatness in you which is seeking to manifest. People will not always like how you do the things you do, but don't stop. Don't give up because of the opposition coming your way. Find strength in it because you are doing something right.

1. **Clarity of dream or vision**

You can't become great if your vision, dream or purpose is bleak or vague. Clarity is what stirs you on to pursue greatness. Your dream, vision or purpose should be plain and clear. Many people want to be great but not many have been able to define their dreams. Their purpose is still unclear to them and some do not have any vision at all. That is a mediocre life. Greatness is not affordable. It is dear. It will manifest if you take time to define and know these things like your life depends on them. If you want to know if you are on the path to greatness, check these. Are your visions clear to you, or do they seem bizarre? Do you know your purpose? What is your dream? People who have clarity on these are more likely to live well and become great because they are guided. You won't jump on anything that comes your way if you are clear on your goals, visions, and dreams.

3. **Rejection and Neglect**

Have you ever felt rejected before? Rejection comes with a feeling of being unwanted, inadequate and mistaken. It can be draining. We often don't like it because it has a negative impression on it. Yet, it is not always the case. I agree with the words of Bo Bennett that *"A rejection is nothing more than a necessary step in the pursuit of success."* Unless you don't want to pursue greatness, rejection will hang around you for a while. Many people have stopped on the path of greatness because of rejection but many others have also jumped this hurdle. On the journey to greatness, rejection cannot be done away with. Yes, it can be frustrating. You will feel discouraged and stacked but it is not the end. Great ideas, initiatives, people often battle rejection. What it means is that you have something the world is waiting for. Change comes with discomfort and that is why rejection sometimes comes. Your greatness is about making a lot of difference. See beyond the rejection before you and pursue it. You are on the right path. You are going to be great soon. I see it.

4. **Favour**

You are sure to be on the journey to greatness when you can't seem to explain some opportunities that come your way. Listen, greatness opens doors. You don't need to arrive before you see the favour. While you are going on the right path, God will show you favour, and He will cause men to favour you also. You will be favoured because you are cut for a great task which you are working on. There will be no favour if you are idle and hoarding all the talents and potentials in you. It doesn't work that way. You are being lazy if you sit unconcerned and unmotivated. If you have made a move, a door will open, men will come to your aid, opportunities will abound and support will come amidst many trials. These will push you into another level of excellence so that your greatness can manifest. In the midst of challenges, favour will be shown to you if you are journeying to greatness. The story of Joseph shows us a lot about greatness.

"But while Joseph was there in the prison, the Lord was with him; he showed him kindness and granted him favour in the eyes of the prison warden. So the warden put Joseph in charge

of all those held in the prison, and he was made responsible for all that was done there. The warden paid no attention to anything under Joseph's care because the Lord was with Joseph and gave him success in whatever he did."

Genesis 39:20b-23

He found favour even in prison. Isn't that amazing? What a great man. Being in prison was part of the journey to greatness for him. Thus, he was favoured at a point where many would be doomed.

5. **Destiny helpers**

Men are helpers. God has made human beings helpers to one another. You can't journey to greatness alone. It is not a solo journey. With all the challenges, opposition and rejection that come with it, it can feel very lonely and discouraging. But here's the good thing; you are never alone. On the journey to greatness, there are helpers to relieve you of the burden. They are those referred to as destiny helpers. Destiny helpers hardly go to the rescue of people who are doing nothing. It is those who are consciously working and moving who receive this help to make the journey successful. They may come in the form of friends, colleagues, family or even strangers. Anybody can be a destiny helper. Recognize that and treat relationships with care. Have you identified any destiny helper yet?

CHAPTER FIVE

Defy the Odds; Dare for Greatness

If something is important enough, even if the odds are against you, you would still do it

Elon Musk

Mediocrity is expensive, and so is greatness. Yet the prices to pay for both are different. It is what distinguishes one from the other. People who become great move out of their comfort zones to get things done. If greatness were easy, it wouldn't even be a subject of discussion. Of course, then everybody would be great and talking about wouldn't be necessary. But greatness isn't easy. It is work! It requires that you go against the odds, a lot of the time, in order to make it.

According to the Collins Dictionary, "*if something happens against all odds, it happens or succeeds although it seemedimpossible or very unlikely*". Many times, greatness requires that you be courageous and make bold decisions even when it seems risky and impossible. Do extraordinary things. Make up your mind to go beyond average, go beyond normal because normalcy is what most people settle for, which doesn't make them great. Greatness is possible, defy the odds and achieve it. Educational challenges, family issues, relationships and financial hardships can make greatness seem far-fetched but these issues can become obstacles that are surmountable. They are not greater than you. You have what it takes to overcome.

Let's look at how to defy all odds and become great.

1. **Focus and consistency.**

Focusing and consistency are two of the most difficult things to maintain. Yet they pay more than they cost when you maintain them. It is easy to be distracted, and also easy to be inconsistent. For greatness to be manifested, you have to be focused and determined. Set your mind on the goal you have; your purpose, dream and vision. Life will be tough. Things won't go as planned but dare...keep on keeping on and you will see the manifestation of the greatness in you. Show me a man who is focused and consistent regardless of boisterous winds against his progress in life and I will show you a man who is on his way to greatness.

1. **Hold on to your values and principles**

Your values and principles are what will keep you when the going gets tough in life. Whether it is integrity, justice, excellence, honesty or loyalty, values define us, keep us on track and guide us to become better persons, help us to make better decisions and increase our confidence. If you don't have any personal values or principles in life, you can walk blindly. There are days when you will be tried and tested, things will look impossible, hold on to your values. A man who holds on to his values is more likely to be greater than one who doesn't. They don't compromise on values and principles easily. Show me a man who won't compromise on his godly values and principles and I will show you a man who is on his way to greatness.

3. Serve!

Service is a powerful weapon that many people despise. It is easy to underestimate its potency. Naturally, humans have ego and love to be served. The few people who commit themselves to service to God and mankind make it to the top. Service will open doors for you and take you places. One of the things that make you great is service. It is a rare activity but very worth it. It requires humility to be served. And humility is needed for greatness.

"Whoever then humbles himself as this child, he is the greatest in the kingdom of heaven.

Matthew 18:4

Jesus reveals to His disciples that the key to being great in His kingdom is humility. This is true and applicable to greatness in our world too. Learn to serve even when it doesn't look promising. Out of that, you will be favoured. Serve God and man, too. You will certainly be rewarded. When the journey becomes tough and there seems to be no hope, consider doing this. Do it wholeheartedly and diligently. You will reap the benefits thereof. As faithful as God is, He rewards those who honour Him by their service. Shungrumbling or complaining when serving and consider all your services as unto the Lord (Colossians 3:23). When the time is due, God will make a way for you. Show me a man who loves to serve God and humanity selflessly and I will show you a man who is on his way to greatness.

4. Let Love Lead

The Word of God requires us to love everybody, whether they deserve it or not. This can be really tough, sometimes, but we have to. Love is what makes every kind of relationship sustainable. Love makes our world better and life easier. Our greatness is not complete without love. In our quest to become great, we need to let love lead. We need to maintain relationships because they can make or unmake us in life.

5. **Fear God**

"The fear of the Lord is the beginning of wisdom: and the knowledge of the holy is understanding" **(Proverbs 9:10)**

God is the giver of wisdom. Everything we need to make it in life can be found in God. If we reverence, we get wisdom for life.

6. **Do The Will of God**

God's will for us is to be great. But not many people choose His will for their lives. Many times, His will is not what we wish for. It is often the opposite of what we desire. It takes complete faith and willingness to walk in His will for our lives. God's will will launch us into our respective places of greatness. If you walk in His will, you will be great. Speak to Him today, read His Word, and know His will for you. That said, follow His plan for your life and you will see the manifestation of your greatness. Show me a man who seeks to do the will of God and I will show you a man who is on his way to Greatness.

7. **Learn to forgive easily.**

Forgiveness is a necessity in life. God's word admonishes us to forgive offenders but the reality of life is that people will hurt us and the consequences of not forgiving can be dire. On your journey to greatness, you will need to forgive the many people who will offend you. Failure to do so can affect your heart and attitude, your productivity and your relationships with people. A man who is serious about attaining greatness is a man who easily forgives and lets go.

8. **Win souls for Christ**

Soul winning is important to God and His kingdom. People who win souls for Christ are seen as great in the kingdom because soul winning is the heartbeat of God. The more you commit yourself to win souls for Christ, the greater you become. Show me a man who wins souls for Christ and I will show you a man who is on his way to greatness.

9. **Sacrifice**

There's one unique feature about people who desire to be great; sacrifice. Sacrifice is a tough thing to do but the people who do it, always reap the benefit thereof. They are ever ready to pay the price. Show me a man who is ever ready to pay the price and I will show you a man who is on his way to greatness.

10. **Time consciousness**

Time is a resource that makes life better or worse, depending on how we use it. It is such a significant tool for restructuring and organizing our plans. We can't control time but we can make good use of it. We can save it, manage, master the use of it and we can also misuse it.

Great people are the ones who pay much attention to time. They utilize it and understand how important it is to becoming great. They recognize that every passing minute cannot be regained if not used wisely. They also acknowledge that opportunities are time-bound. A man who values time is one who is on his way to greatness. Such a man makes judicious use of their time.

Conclusions

Your greatness will manifest only when you work towards it. It is said that Rome was not built in a day. Great things do not happen in a day nor does the manifestation of greatness. Go through the process, don't rush it and watch God make it happen. Remember that greatness can also be increased. There is more room for you to increase. You don't have to stop where you are, reach for more in God.

"You will increase my greatness and comfort me on every side" **Psalm 71:21.**

Greatness can come from unusual, unassuming people and places. Some people do not look promising, but that doesn't mean they can't be great. Greatness can come from anywhere. Remember the story about Nazareth in the Bible?

"Can anything good come from Nazareth?' "Come and see for yourself" **(John 45-46).**

Nazareth was an obscure village. It was despised by the Jews because a Roman army garrison was located there. Some have speculated that an aloof attitude or a poor reputation in morals and religion on the part of the people of Nazareth led to Nathanael's harsh comment. So, Nathanael could not fathom that a significant and great person as the Messiah would come from such an insignificant place as Nazareth. But eventually, greatness came out of Nazareth.

- **Perez's breakthrough was unexpected.**

There are times when greatness takes many by surprise. Greatness is worked at but its manifestation can be incredibly shocking. It can take many people by surprise. The story of Perez's breakthrough at birth shows how unexpected greatness can be. His twin brother, Zerah's hand had emerged first at birth but in the end, it was Perez who came forth first. (Gen 38:29–30; 1 Chronicles 2:4). It was so unexpected. Greatness can be too. It doesn't really matter where you find yourself in life, if you believe, allow God and commit yourself to working on yourself and your dreams, you can be great. The seed of greatness is in you. Believe it. You are great.

When we read the story of God's great people in the Bible, we can feel their greatness and sometimes we wonder if we can do or become much as they did. The good news is that now, we can do much more than the people of old whose stories inspire us. Jesus, after completing his assignment on earth said that we, those who would come to believe in Him will do greater things. *"Greater works than these shall you do because I go to my Father. God always wants us to do greater, all the time".* We have all we need to outdo what the great people in the past did or become.

Your gifts and talents will cause your greatness to manifest. God gives us gifts and talents so that we can use them to make an impact wherever we find ourselves. Find what it is and use it. It is said that it is your attitude, not your aptitude that determines your altitude in life. Your approach to life and people can influence how great you can become.

"According as his divine power hath given unto us all things that pertain unto life and godliness, through the knowledge of him that hath called us to glory and virtue:" **2 Peter 1:3.**

God has done His part. It is time for you to do your part also so that your manifestation can come swiftly. You are made for greatness. There is greatness in you. Don't stop where you are. Don't grow weary. Don't give up. Just keep pressing because your season of manifestation is here. You are such a great person. The world is waiting for your manifestation.

9 798887 838267

Printed by Libri Plureos GmbH in Hamburg,
Germany